Sea...ns

Katie Orchard

HODDER
Wayland

an ir

Titles in this series:
Seaside Towns
Villages

For more information on this series and other Hodder Wayland titles, go to www.hodderwayland.co.uk

Exploring Seaside Towns is a simplified and updated version of Hodder Wayland's *Landmarks: Exploring Seaside Towns*

Text copyright © Hodder Wayland 2004
Volume copyright © Hodder Wayland 2004

Editor: Katie Sergeant
Designers: Tim Mayer and Malcolm Walker
Typesetter: Jane Hawkins
Cover Design: Hodder Children's Books

First published in 1997 by Wayland Publishers Ltd.
Updated and published in 2004 by Hodder Wayland, an imprint of Hodder Children's Books
This paperback edition published in 2005

Orchard, Katie
  Exploring seaside towns
  1. Seaside resorts - Great Britain - Juvenile literature
  2. Seaside resorts - Great Britain - History - Juvenile literature
  3. Vacations - Great Britain - Juvenile literature
  4. Vacations - Great Britain - History - Juvenile literature
  I. Title
  307.7'6'0941
  ISBN 075024612X

Printed in China

Hodder Children's Books
A division of Hodder Headline Limited
338 Euston Road, London NW1 3BH

Cover: Painted houses in Tobermory, Isle of Mull, Scotland; **inset picture:** A fisherman removing crabs from a crab pot aboard a fishing boat.
Title page: Salcombe, South Devon, is a popular destination for British tourists.
Contents: Small boats moor in the harbour at Ilfracombe, North Devon.

Picture acknowledgements:
Cover: (inset) Alamy/ Stephen Bond, (main) Corbis/ Niall Benvie.
Charles Barker plc: 36 (bottom); Jennie Chapman: 11 (top), 21 (bottom), 22 (bottom), 25; Essex County Council, David Bartam: 24 (top); Eye Ubiquitous: 14 (top), 22 (top), 34 (top), 40/ AJG Bell 33 (top)/ Davy Bold 28/ Davey Boyle 23/ Sylvia Greenland 13/ Stephen Rafferty 18 (top)/ Paul Thompson, contents page, 4 (top), 32, 37 (bottom); Pat and Martin Fitzgerald: 19 (both); Hodder Wayland Picture Library: 18 (bottom), 21 (top), 30 (bottom); Phil Holden: 36 (top); Impact Photos: Alan Blair 15, 35/ Mark Cator 8/ Piers Cavendish title page, 38/ Stuart Clarke 33 (bottom)/ Michael Good 5/ Chris Moyse 34 (bottom)/ Tony Page 10, 16 (top)/ David Reed 4 (bottom), 39/ Roger Scrutton 31/ Simon Shepheard 6/ Homer Sykes 12, 14 (bottom), 16 (bottom)/ Francesca Yorke 20 (both); Isle of White County Press: 41; The Lowestoft Journal: 17; The Mayflower County Primary School, Harwich: 24 (bottom); Mary Evans Picture Library: 11 (bottom), 13; Public Records Office: 30 (top); St Luke's Junior School, Brighton: 26 (both); Mark Smales: 9 (both); Paul Taverner: 29 (top); Trinity House: 29 (bottom). The artwork on pages 7, 10, 27, 43 and 47 is by Peter Bull.

Every effort has been made to contact the people featured in the case studies of the original version of this book, and to check the facts and figures. If any factual details are now incorrect, the Publisher will make the necessary changes in any further reprintings of this title.

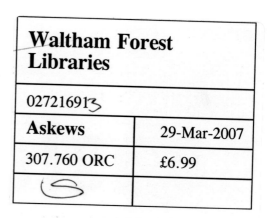

Contents

Words in **bold** can be found in the glossary.

What is a Seaside Town?

Seaside towns are not just places to visit on holiday. Many people live and work in seaside towns, all year round.

With 15,000 kilometres of coastline, the UK has many seaside towns. Some are small fishing ports, such as Mousehole, in Cornwall. Others are large, bustling tourist resorts, such as Blackpool, in Lancashire.

▲ Small fishing boats moor safely in the old fishing port of Brixham, in Devon.

◄ Many seaside towns are in areas of outstanding natural beauty, such as the Giant's Causeway, near Portrush, in Northern Ireland.

The UK has a varied coastline, with many different types of seaside town. Many of the oldest towns were once small fishing ports or naval bases, built around natural **harbours** or **estuaries**. Some seaside towns have grown up along dramatic **headlands** or cliffs, such as the famous 'white cliffs' of Dover. Others were built around sheltered bays. Some beaches are sandy and others are made up of pebbles.

Families enjoy a day out on Portobello beach, near Edinburgh, Scotland. ▼

SEASIDE POPULATIONS

TOWN	POPULATION
Ardglass, County Down	1,700
Tenby, Wales	5,000
St Ives, Cornwall	9,500
St Andrews, Fife	14,500
Skegness, Lincolnshire	17,000

Many seaside **settlements** have features that are not found elsewhere. Piers, **promenades**, lighthouses, old stone **harbours** and modern marinas are important seaside landmarks. Some towns are built either side of an **estuary**, and have bridges linking one side of a town to another. Others have **causeways**, areas of land that can only be crossed when the tide goes out.

WEATHER PATTERNS

Average rainfall (mm) in June 2003

| Eskdalemuir   100 | Bognor Regis   34 |
| (W. Scotland) | (S. England) |

Average sunshine (hours per day) in June 2003

| Eskdalemuir   3 | Bognor Regis   8 |

A seaside pier, like the one in Brighton, is a dramatic landmark that can be seen from all around. ▼

Seaside weather

For most people, the weather plays an important part in deciding where to spend their holidays. In the summer, the north and west of the UK have the most rainfall. The south and east tend to have more sunshine. But the weather in the UK can change quickly from day to day. Many people now spend their holidays abroad, where the weather is more likely to be warm. Many UK resorts are improving leisure facilities to make sure that they continue to attract tourists, whatever the weather.

This map of Scarborough shows just some of the activities that you can do there. ▼

ACTIVITY

Imagine you are visiting Scarborough. Use this map to plan a fun day out for you and your family. What activities could you do if the weather was bad?

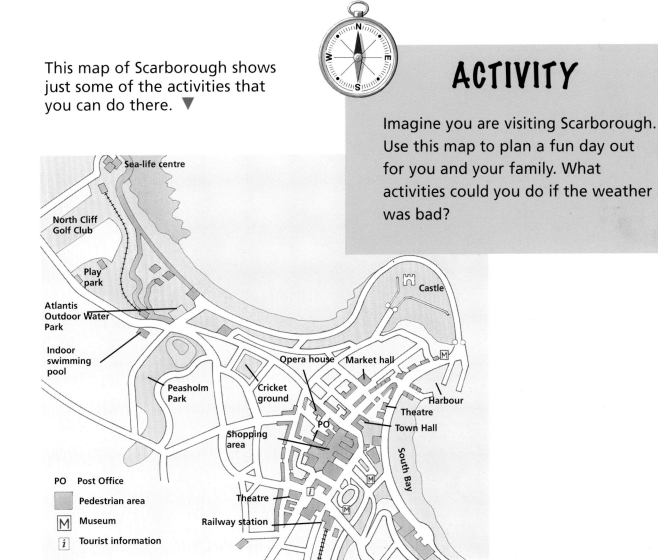

Sea-life centre

North Cliff Golf Club

Play park

Atlantis Outdoor Water Park

Indoor swimming pool

Peasholm Park

Cricket ground

Opera house

Market hall

Castle

Harbour

Theatre

Town Hall

Shopping area

PO

South Bay

Theatre

Railway station

PO   Post Office

Pedestrian area

M   Museum

i   Tourist information

Seaside Life

▲ Newquay, in Cornwall, has been a bustling tourist resort since **Victorian** times.

It may be difficult to imagine, but most large seaside resorts were once small fishing villages. The people who lived there relied on the sea for food and for work. Fishermen sold part of their catch to people living inland, and kept the rest to feed their families. In some seaside towns, the fishermen's cottages are still standing today.

Flamborough Lifeboat Crew

For about 180 years crews of the Royal National Lifeboat Institute (RNLI) all over the UK have rescued people from danger out at sea. Today, there are lifeboat stations in many seaside towns.

▲ Flamborough lifeboat crew.

The crew at Flamborough Lifeboat Station is made up of volunteers. They each carry a bleeper, which tells them when there is an emergency at sea. When the bleeper goes off, the first three people to arrive at the station go out to the rescue.

The crew uses an Atlantic 75 lifeboat – a fast boat that is equipped to go out in the roughest of weather.

Three members of the Flamborough lifeboat crew head off at top speed to a rescue. ▶

Some coastal **settlements** began as defence posts. In **Norman times,** castles and watchtowers were built along the south-east coast of England to spot invaders approaching.

A new trend

In the eighteenth century, the **Prince Regent** made it fashionable for rich people to visit the seaside. People at the time believed that drinking sea water was good for their health. They did not swim in the sea, but sometimes they were dipped in it by special servants called 'dippers'. Rich people flocked to seaside towns and built grand houses, many of which are still standing today.

PRINCE REGENT'S HEALTH CURE RECIPE

◊ Sea water mixed with milk
◊ Cream of tartar
◊ Crabs eyes
◊ Snakeskin
◊ Woodlice

▲ Some of the 'cures' were pretty revolting!

This is a typical **Regency** seaside terrace in Brighton. ▼

▲ In **Victorian** times, bathing machines waited to take tourists into the sea on Brighton beach.

It was not until Victorian times that seaside towns became tourist resorts. In those days, men and women could not swim on the same beach at the same time. Swimming costumes were heavy, and covered swimmers from head to toe. And people were taken into the sea in huge, horse-drawn bathing machines!

This Regency cartoon shows Scarborough's famous 'dipper', Widow Tucker. ▶

In Bexhill-on-Sea, East Sussex, the population doubled between 1890 and 1901.

Visitors to Bournemouth enjoy an open-air concert in the park. ▼

Trips to the sea

Before the 1800s, only rich people visited the seaside. With the introduction of railways in the 1840s, railway tracks soon snaked all over the country. This made it easier for more people to visit the coast. Many seaside towns became holiday resorts and began to grow quickly. Many nineteenth-century hotels, piers and bandstands are still standing today.

	Resident population	Summer population
Poole, Dorset	138,000	Over 2 million
Portrush, County Antrim	5,000	Over 25,000

Changing populations

During the summer, the population of a seaside town can grow enormously, with the arrival of thousands of tourists. Visitors to seaside towns provide jobs for the people who live there. Many work in hotels, cafés, restaurants or tourist attractions. But this work may only last during the busy summer period. In small seaside towns, some local businesses close down during the winter.

Seaside names

The name of a seaside town may give clues about its past. Some names show the age of the town – Scarborough was named after the tenth-century Viking, Thorgils Skarthi. Other names have a royal connection, such as Bognor Regis – 'Regis' means 'belonging to a king'.

During the eighteenth and nineteenth centuries, Lyme Regis was popular with royal visitors, so 'Regis' was added to its name. ▶

▲ Houses in Aberystwyth, in Wales, nestle between the sea and a backdrop of dramatic hills.

Seaside homes

With the sea on one side, and protected countryside behind them, many seaside towns have grown up along a narrow strip of coastline. In most resorts older homes are usually in the centre of the town or on the seafront. More modern housing has then built up around them.

Many people live in high-rise flats, with **balconies** looking out to sea. Seaside towns attract many retired people, who choose to sell their city homes and move to the coast. There are often rest homes and retirement flats.

◀ Bournemouth's warm climate has always attracted retired people.

Many grand **Regency** houses have now been divided up into smaller flats. Some are spacious, but others can be very cramped.

Living by the sea has its own problems. In popular resorts, rents and house prices can be high. This makes it difficult for local people to find an affordable home. Houses by the sea may flood in bad weather. Sea winds and salty air can attack the outside paintwork.

ACTIVITY

Every kind of **settlement** has good and bad features. Make a list of the problems and attractions in your area. Think about what you would like to change.

During the winter, strong winds and rough seas batter Scarborough's seafront. ▼

Work

Today, people who live in seaside towns do the same kind of jobs as people living in any other type of **settlement**. They work in shops, offices, schools, hospitals and the tourist industry. But about 250 years ago, almost every family living in seaside towns was involved in fishing or sailing.

▲ Many old fishing boats now take tourists on day trips.

Building a wooden boat the traditional way. ▼

The fishing industry once employed many thousands of people. Today, the industry is in **decline**.

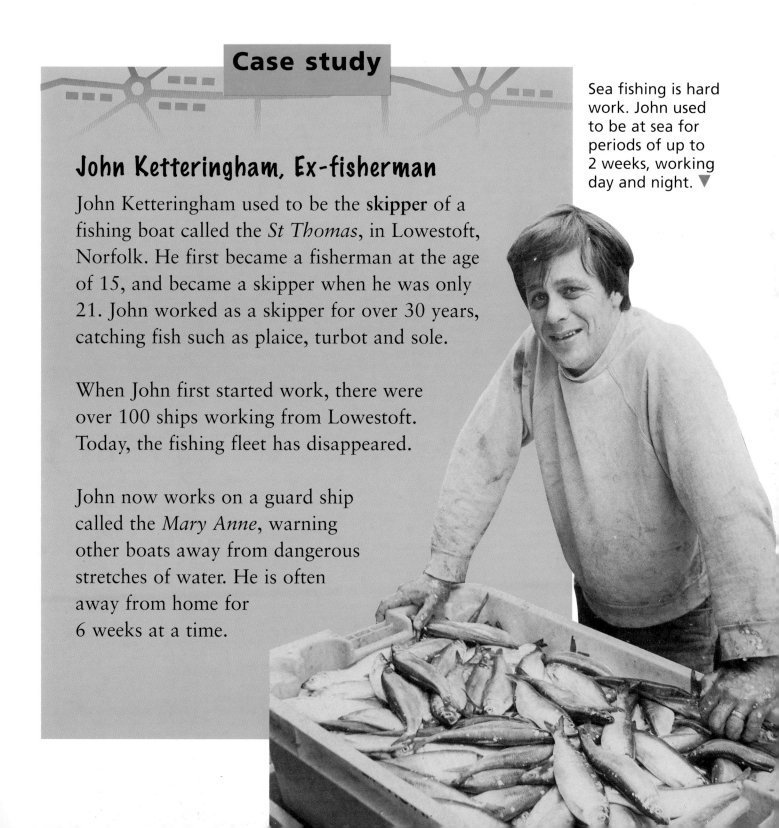

Case study

John Ketteringham, Ex-fisherman

John Ketteringham used to be the **skipper** of a fishing boat called the *St Thomas*, in Lowestoft, Norfolk. He first became a fisherman at the age of 15, and became a skipper when he was only 21. John worked as a skipper for over 30 years, catching fish such as plaice, turbot and sole.

When John first started work, there were over 100 ships working from Lowestoft. Today, the fishing fleet has disappeared.

John now works on a guard ship called the *Mary Anne*, warning other boats away from dangerous stretches of water. He is often away from home for 6 weeks at a time.

Sea fishing is hard work. John used to be at sea for periods of up to 2 weeks, working day and night. ▼

Tourism

The growth of the tourist industry created lots of new jobs in seaside towns. Hotels, restaurants, shops and theatres all sprang up in these areas, providing work for local people.

Seasonal work

Some jobs in seaside towns are only available during the busy summer months. This type of work is called **seasonal work**. **Chambermaids**, lifeguards and deckchair attendants usually have seasonal jobs during the summer.

▲ Many beach lifeguards work for only a few months a year.

Hotel chambermaids are kept very busy during the tourist season. ▶

The Trevelyan Hotel, Penzance

Pat and Martin Fitzgerald ran the Trevelyan Hotel in Penzance for 18 years. The bed and breakfast was in an eighteenth-century building only 2 minutes walk from the sea.

Running a small family business is hard work. The hotel was open all year round, but it was busiest during the summer. A temporary chambermaid was employed during the tourist season to keep the eight bedrooms tidy. Pat used to get up early to cook breakfast for her guests. She used to cook more than 4,500 eggs each year!

Pat and Martin retired in 2002. ▶

▲ The Trevelyan Hotel was in one of the most historic areas of Penzance, in Cornwall.

Unemployment

Many seaside towns have come to depend on tourism to provide work for people living there. In many places the tourist trade only provides **seasonal work**. The number of jobs available depends on the number of tourists visiting the area. If tourism **declines**, this often has a knock-on effect on jobs. Many seaside towns have high levels of unemployment. Local people often have to travel long distances to get to work. Some people leave the area altogether.

▲ This shopping street in the old part of Hastings is popular with tourists, who spend money in the area.

◀ These old fishermen's cottages in Hastings are now fast-food restaurants.

New jobs

Some local councils are working hard to encourage new businesses to move to seaside towns. In coastal areas, it is important to attract organisations that can provide employment for people all year round. Shops, banks and insurance companies have all sprung up in larger seaside towns, creating jobs for local people.

Case study

In-line Skating Coach

'Blade Marc' works as an in-line skating coach on the seafront in Hove, East Sussex. He has taught people from the ages of 5 to 75 how to skate!

In-line skating is very popular in Hove with tourists and residents alike. Hove seafront is an ideal place to practise the sport, because it has a long, wide, smooth **promenade**. During the summer months, the promenade is busy with wobbly beginners and polished expert skaters, all enjoying the sport by the sea.

'Blade Marc' practises on Hove seafront. ▶

Some of the larger tourist resorts, such as Bournemouth and Brighton, now have conference centres that are used for big meetings and even live concerts. They provide all-year-round employment and entertainment for local people.

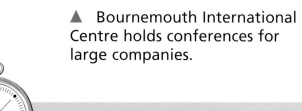
▲ Bournemouth International Centre holds conferences for large companies.

ACTIVITY

Ask your family and friends to show you photographs of their holidays by the sea. Look out for people working in the background and see how many different types of jobs you can spot. Try making a collage of your own holiday photographs, showing different types of seaside work.

◀ These holiday photos were taken on Brighton Pier.

Although Brighton is a popular tourist resort, only a small percentage of its workforce have jobs in the tourist industry. About 10 per cent work in hotels and catering. Many people work in the **service industry**, in shops, banks, and restaurants.

Some seaside towns have built sports facilities, creating new jobs and offering water sports to visitors, such as windsurfing and jet-skiing. Many larger towns do not depend solely on tourism to provide jobs. For instance, Poole, in Dorset, has a busy harbour and runs passenger ferry services to and from France.

Tourists in Poole climb aboard a small boat for a trip round the harbour. ▼

Seaside Schools

There is no such thing as a typical seaside school. They are as varied as the seaside towns themselves. What they do have in common is their connection with the sea. For example, the Mayflower County Primary School in Dovercourt, Harwich, takes its name from a ship called the *Mayflower*, which took some of the first settlers to America in 1620.

This painting shows some of the early settlers leaving Plymouth, about to board the *Mayflower*. ▶

◀ The infant playground at the Mayflower school in Harwich.

Seaside Carnival

Every year, pupils at King Offa Primary School, in Bexhill-on-Sea, take part in the town's summer carnival. People from the whole community take part in this colourful event. There is a procession, with music, clowns and a funfair. The children from King Offa Primary School pick a different theme for their costumes each year.

▲ Pupils from King Offa Primary School dress up as ancient Egyptians for the carnival.

Seaside schools often make the most of being by the sea. Pupils can visit the beach to collect shells and fossils, and learn about sea wildlife. They may also visit local maritime museums that have exhibitions about local history.

Wherever they are built, schools always have an important part to play within the community. Pupils usually live close by and their parents often work in the area.

St Luke's Junior School, in Brighton, makes the most of its location. Pupils can walk to the seafront in just a few minutes. It was built high on a hill overlooking the sea, in 1903.

▲ St Luke's School in Brighton is lucky enough to have a fine view of the sea.

The school is surrounded by lots of **Victorian** buildings. Pupils from the school often investigate the local area to find clues about its Victorian past.

On a field trip, pupils from St Luke's study the Victorian buildings surrounding the school. ▼

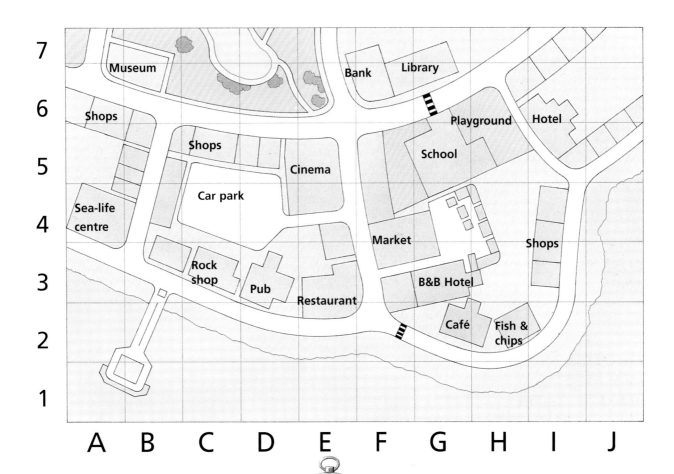

Schoolchildren in seaside towns may get involved in traditional local events. In Whitby, North Yorkshire, the whole town takes part in the 'Blessing of the Boats' ceremony. People in the town have performed the ceremony for centuries, praying for the safe return of boats.

ACTIVITY

The grid map above shows a typical seaside town. The co-ordinate for the rock shop is C3. Using the letters and numbers on the grid, find the co-ordinates for the sea-life centre, the pub and the bed and breakfast (B&B). Turn to page 46 to check your answers. Draw a grid map of your local area and write down the co-ordinates for important landmarks.

Transport

Seaside towns need good transport links to thrive, allowing visitors to be able to reach them easily.

Seaside ports

Many of today's seaside towns were once seaports. These ports were the main ways of entering and leaving the country.

Today, seaports are still used by ships to carry goods and passengers across the Channel. In Folkstone, Kent, the Channel Tunnel provides a fast, underwater link for cars, lorries and trains to the rest of Europe.

The Wightlink ferry service transports people and goods between the Isle of Wight and the mainland. ▶

Southwold Lighthouse

In many seaside towns, lighthouses are important landmarks, guiding boats safely round the coast. Southwold Lighthouse in Suffolk was built right on the seafront in 1889.

Keith Seaman is the lighthouse attendant. He looks after the equipment and makes sure that everything is running smoothly. He also takes tours round the lighthouse on two afternoons a week. The lantern used to be powered by oil, pumped to the top of the tower by hand. Today, it is powered by electricity and controlled by a computer.

"The light can be seen as far as 35 kilometres out to sea, and it is as bright as 47,000 candles!" says Keith.

It is Keith's job to make sure that all the equipment in the lighthouse is working properly. ▶

▲ The lighthouse is 31 metres high. Keith has to climb a spiral staircase with 99 steps to reach the top.

▲ An old poster advertising rail trips to Skegness.

The railway age

Some of the UK's oldest seaside resorts are close to large cities. When steam-powered trains were introduced, it became easier for people in these cities to get to the seaside on the growing railway network and so the resorts became more popular.

In the 1920s and 1930s, railways were run by electricity. This made them even faster and meant that journey times were shorter. More and more people travelled from the cities to the coast on the train.

▲ The **Park-and-Ride** scheme in Brighton encourages people to use the bus instead of their cars.

ACTIVITY

Carry out your own traffic survey to see which are the busiest times of the day where you live. Take an adult with you and stand in a safe spot by a main road. Count the number of vehicles that pass by. Record the amount of traffic at different times of the day in a table or graph and compare your results. You may find it useful to make a table of different types of transport, such as buses, cars and bicycles.

Traffic solutions

Today, more people travel by car than by train. In some seaside towns, **planners** have introduced Park-and-Ride schemes to encourage drivers to park their cars outside the town and travel to the centre by bus.

Unusual vehicles

Some seaside towns have unusual types of transport. Open-top buses and **trams** allow tourists to do sight-seeing while they travel. There are also **funicular railways**. In towns built on **estuaries**, people can travel by ferry from one part of the town to the other.

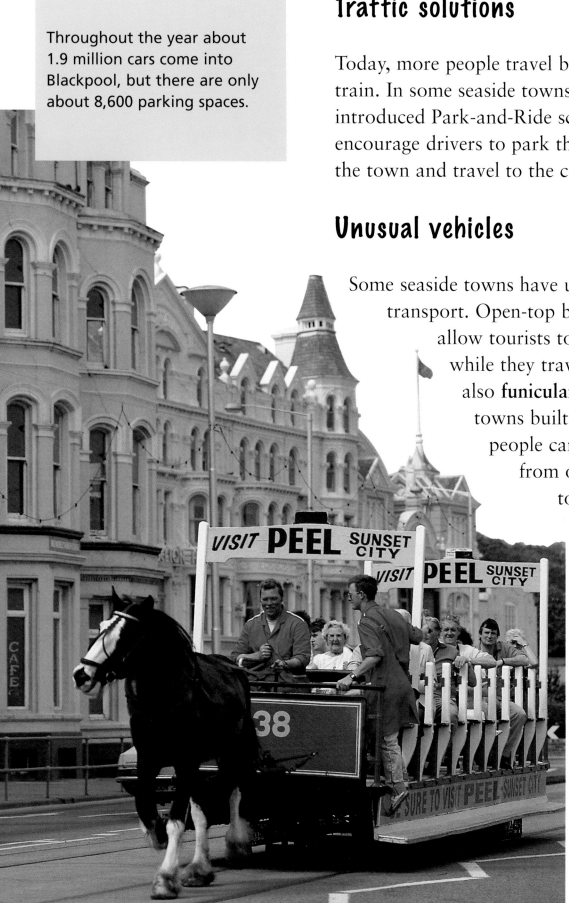

Throughout the year about 1.9 million cars come into Blackpool, but there are only about 8,600 parking spaces.

◀ A horse-drawn tram in Douglas, Isle of Man.

Shops and Entertainment

Most seaside towns have lots of things for visitors to do. Swimming, sunbathing, and spending the day on the beach are all fun parts of a trip to the seaside. Traditional activities, such as donkey rides and Punch and Judy shows, are still popular with tourists. Modern attractions, such as sea-life centres and water sports, also add to the fun of a seaside holiday.

Tourist shops along the seafront sell all kinds of souvenirs, from postcards and buckets and spades, to local crafts and antiques. Food stalls sell seafood, ice creams and candyfloss, and there are always plenty of restaurants to choose from.

Children enjoy a donkey ride on
Skegness beach, in Lincolnshire. ▼

Piers

During **Victorian** and **Edwardian** times, over 100 piers were built along the coasts of resorts in England and Wales. They were made from cast iron and wood. Many have been lost, but 55 are still standing today, although some are not in use. Piers are still popular with visitors, who enjoy eating fish and chips, playing games in amusement arcades and going on fairground rides.

▲ Many seaside towns have their own funfair.

Southend Pier is the UK's longest pier, at 3.4 kilometres.

Brighton Pier is the busiest, attracting over 3.5 million visitors each year.

◄ Many seaside stalls sell sweets, sticks of rock and candyfloss.

With cheap air travel and the likelihood of warmer weather, more and more people are now choosing to take their holidays abroad. Competition from foreign resorts means that many seaside towns have to work much harder to attract visitors. **Planners** try to improve facilities, by building new swimming pools, skateboard areas, volleyball pitches, funfairs and sports facilities all over the UK.

▲ Sea-life centres attract tourists, whatever the weather.

ACTIVITY

Postcards make good souvenirs after a trip to the seaside. Design a postcard of the area where you live. Show the most attractive features to encourage tourists to visit.

Tourists choose postcards in Perranporth, in Cornwall. ▶

Tourism all year round

Many seaside towns now have attractions that can be visited all year round. Maritime museums, heritage sites, buildings of historical importance and nature reserves are all open to the public. They encourage people to visit the area and provide steady jobs for local people. For example, the old fishing town of Whitby, in North Yorkshire, is in an area called the 'Heritage Coast'. Tourists are encouraged to visit the many sites of historical interest in this area.

Whitby attracts many fans of the novel, *Dracula*. The author, Bram Stoker, set many of his stories there. ▼

▲ A surfer catches a wave in Newquay, in Cornwall. This is part of the area known as 'Surfers' Paradise'.

Sports

Surfing, body boarding and sailing are just a few of the sports available in seaside towns. Visitors can also hire boats for sea fishing and diving. Some seaside towns host international sporting events, including golf tournaments in St Andrews, in Scotland, and the TT Motorcycle Race in Douglas, Isle of Man.

Places to stay

Some large seaside resorts attract millions of visitors every year. Visitors stay in a wide range of accommodation, including hotels, 'bed and breakfasts', caravans, holiday cottages, or in tents on campsites.

Holiday camps employ people to entertain children staying there. ▶

Blackpool Pleasure Beach and Tower

Blackpool Pleasure Beach first opened in 1896. This popular amusement park has rides to suit people of all ages.

Amusements include five wooden roller-coasters, including the 'Big Dipper', which was built in 1923. The world-famous 'Pepsi Max – the Big One', which opened in 1994, is a terrifying, 1,675.5-metre-long roller-coaster ride, travelling at speeds of 119 kph! 'Valhalla' opened in 2000 and it is the world's largest ride in the dark.

The Blackpool Tower was built in 1894 and is over 158 metres high. Two lifts take visitors right to the top, where there is a postbox for sending postcards home.

▲ The famous Blackpool Tower is over 100 years old.

Donkey rides are still a popular attraction on Blackpool beach. ▶

Seaside Towns and Change

With so much competition from holiday resorts abroad, seaside towns need to change with the times to continue to thrive.

Planners have to develop facilities to attract visitors and provide employment for local people all year round. But it is important that new buildings do not spoil the beautiful environment that people come to see. There has to be a balance between keeping the good things about seaside towns and making changes to improve them.

Coastal walks attract millions of hikers each year. But if too many people walk in an area they can damage pathways. ▶

The number of young people living in seaside towns is rising. Planners need to invest money in more low-cost housing to provide suitable homes for single people and young families.

Protecting coasts

The shape of the UK's coastline is also under threat. Coasts are battered constantly by the weather and the sea. Many cliffs are being eroded, or worn away, by wind, rain and snow. Sea defences have been built in many coastal areas to protect the coastline.

Wooden sea defences like these can stop the sea from eroding cliffs. ▼

Work is being done to protect the natural environment of many coastal **settlements**. Environmental organisations are working hard to prevent **erosion** and damage to coastlines from new development, as well as caring for local wildlife.

This bird colony of cormorants, gannets and gulls in Northumberland is now a protected area. ▶

Pollution

A major cause of coastal pollution in the past has been the dumping of untreated human waste into the sea. This is dangerous and can cause health problems for people who swim in the water. Fortunately, the amount of sewage in the sea has decreased over the years. Farm and factory waste also pollutes the sea, but businesses are forced by law to treat their waste products before dumping them.

Many seaside towns are cleaning up their beaches, making them safer for swimmers, but more needs to be done.

Seaside towns are being encouraged to tackle the pollution problem. The Blue Flag Campaign compares UK resorts with similar ones in Europe. The cleanest beaches receive a Blue Flag Award. In 2003, 105 UK beaches were given the award.

A young protester makes her point with a banner. ▼

Surfers Against Sewage (SAS)

For 13 years, a group of protesters known as Surfers Against Sewage (SAS) has campaigned against the pumping of raw sewage into the sea. Today, thanks to groups like this one, far less sewage is allowed to enter UK waters, and many more beaches have received Blue Flag Awards.

SAS has now turned its attention towards other forms of coastal pollution, such as chemical and nuclear pollution. In September 2002, 3,000 surfers attended a fancy-dress ball in St Agnes, in Cornwall, to protest against pollution.

I WANT TO SWIM IN THE SEA NOT IN SEWAGE

Finding Out More

There are many ways to find out more about a seaside town.

See for yourself

Many seaside towns have tourist information offices, with brochures and leaflets packed full of things to do in the area. These will tell you about local history and important landmarks. Local newspapers provide articles about daily life.

Ask around

Your local library may have all kinds of information about seaside towns. The librarian will be able to help you find maps, reference books, magazines and newspapers.

The planning department of the local council can send you information about future plans for the area. The nearest County Record Office will have old maps and records showing how things have changed in the area over time.

The Internet

If you have access to a computer, the Internet can provide all kinds of information about a particular seaside town, including the shops, hotels, restaurants and tourist attractions in the area.

Maps

Several different types of map will give you information about an area. A road atlas will show where a town is in the UK. Street plans give a little more information and can sometimes be found in a map book covering the whole county. For even more detail, find an Ordnance Survey map of the area.

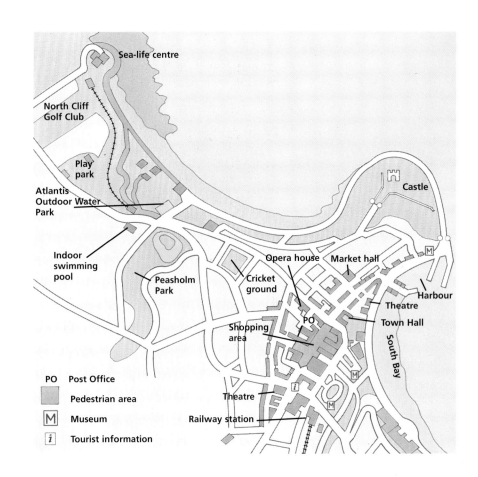

Census information

Census information gives details about how many people live in an area, how old they are, what jobs they do, what type of home they live in and whether or not they own a car. You can find census information in a large public library, or on the Internet.

Places to visit

Tourist information centres, maritime museums, heritage centres and sea-life centres.

Seaside scrapbook

Once you have collected all your information, you can make a scrapbook of your chosen seaside town. Include leaflets, postcards, photographs, tourist information, maps and tape recordings of interviews.

Notes For Adults

This book is designed to be an introduction to seaside towns and their communities. It looks at various aspects of coastal life, including seaside homes, jobs, schools and entertainment. Many different types of seaside town are explored, and this book can be used by children who live in any type of settlement as a comparative guide.

Case studies in each chapter provide specific information about a particular aspect of life in a seaside town. Children can use this information to make a direct comparison with their own experiences.

This book also includes several simple activities. They have been designed so that children from any type of settlement can attempt them. Some of the activities may demonstrate a particular point that has been made about seaside towns or they may encourage them to use their observational skills. Children are encouraged to use some of the methods employed by geographers to find out information or present data, such as mapping and graph skills, conducting surveys and using primary source material such as interviews or census data.

What is a Seaside Town (pages 4–7)
This chapter gives a brief overview of different types of seaside town found in the UK. The language and examples used encourage children to look around them and either compare or contrast their own settlement with that of a seaside town. The text examines what special features distinguish seaside towns from other types of settlement.

Activity on page 7:
This activity is designed to illustrate how to use a map to extract information about local landmarks. Encourage children to think about the distance they would have to travel to get from one attraction to another, so that they include this in their planning.

Seaside Life (pages 8–15)
This chapter looks at who lives in a seaside town, its key buildings and focal points of seaside life. It also covers the history of seaside towns in the UK.

Activity on page 15:
This activity invites children to think about the advantages and disadvantages of where they live. Ask them why they feel some aspects are better than others. Do they live too far from shops and services? Is there enough for them to do in their spare time? Are there any improvements they would like to make to their local area?

Work (pages 16–23)

This chapter deals with the seaside town economy, including traditional types of employment and how this has changed today. Children are encouraged to think about how the nature of a particular settlement is reflected in the type of employment available in the area.

Activity on page 22:

This activity encourages children to use their own primary source evidence to explore the type of work found in a seaside town. What happens to these jobs in the winter? Is all the work in the area seasonal? Can the children find examples of work that is available all year round?

Seaside Schools (pages 24–27)

This chapter allows children to compare or contrast their own school with the seaside examples in the text.

Activity on page 27:

This mapping activity encourages children to use grid references and co-ordinates to find landmarks on a map. Children are also invited to produce a grid map of their own. They can do this for the area around their own school.

Transport (pages 28–31)

In this chapter children are prompted to think about the importance of good transport networks in and around a seaside town. They could also think about the more unusual forms of transport provided for tourists.

Activity on page 30:

Children are invited to think about the amount of traffic on the UK's roads. They can break down their survey into different types of transport counted at different times of the day. Encourage them to use the tallying system of counting.

Shops and Entertainment (pages 32–37)

This chapter shows how the character of a seaside town is reflected in the local shops and facilities, and how these are changing.

Activity on page 34:

This activity invites children to focus on the good points about where they live, and think about what might seem attractive to visitors.

Seaside Towns and Change (pages 38–41)

This chapter demonstrates that whilst seaside towns are attractive places to live, the changing way of life can bring problems, which need to be resolved. It particularly looks at environmental problems.

Finding Out More (pages 42–43)

This section may provide some useful ideas on how to start researching a particular seaside town. It is only intended as a starting point, not as a definitive guide.

Glossary

balconies Platforms outside windows where people can sit.

causeways Areas of land that can only be crossed when the tide is out.

census A survey of the population. It is carried out every ten years.

chambermaid A hotel worker who makes the beds and tidies the guests' rooms.

decline Worsen. In this instance, provided less income.

Edwardian During the reign of King Edward VII (1901–10).

erosion Wearing away of the land.

estuary The part of a river that runs into the sea.

funicular railway A railway that goes up a steep hillside or cliff.

harbours Areas of coast where boats can shelter from the weather.

headland A narrow strip of land jutting out into the sea.

Norman times In the eleventh and twelfth century, after Britain was conquered by the Norman king, William, in 1066.

Park-and-Ride A scheme where people are encouraged to park their cars outside the busy town centre, and catch a regular bus service to get to the shopping area.

planners People that make plans about the future development of an area.

Prince Regent A prince that takes over the role of a king, while the king is still alive, but unable to perform his duties.

promenade A wide walkway that runs along the seafront.

Regency The period between 1811–1820, before the Prince Regent became King George IV.

seasonal work Work that is only available at certain times of the year.

service industry People who work in the service industry sell a service to their customers, rather than making or selling goods.

settlements Places where people live.

skipper The captain of a boat.

trams Passenger vehicles powered by electric cables overhead, which run on rails in the street.

Victorian The period of Queen Victoria's reign (1837–1901).

Answers from p27
Sea-life centre: A4; Pub: D3; B&B: G3

Books To Read

Beside the Sea (Changes) by Liz Gogerly (Hodder Wayland, 2004)

Bustling Coastlines (The Natural World) by Babara Taylor (Ticktock Media, 2003)

Coasts (Earth in Danger) by Polly Goodman (Hodder Wayland, 2005)

Coastlines (Geography First) by Kay Barnham (Hodder Wayland, 2004)

Seaside Holidays (Start-up History) by Stewart Ross (Evans, 2002)

This map shows the main seaside towns mentioned in the text:

1 Aberystwyth
2 Ardglass
3 Bexhill-on-Sea
4 Blackpool
5 Bognor Regis
6 Brighton and Hove
7 Brixham
8 Bournemouth
9 Dover
10 Douglas
11 Eskdalemuir
12 Flamborough
13 Folkstone
14 Harwich
15 Hastings
16 Lowestoft
17 Lyme Regis
18 Mousehole
19 Newquay
20 Penzance
21 Perranporth
22 Poole
23 Portobello beach
24 Portrush
25 Scarborough
26 Skegness
27 Southend
28 Southwold
29 St Agnes
30 St Andrew's
31 St Ives
32 Tenby
33 Whitby

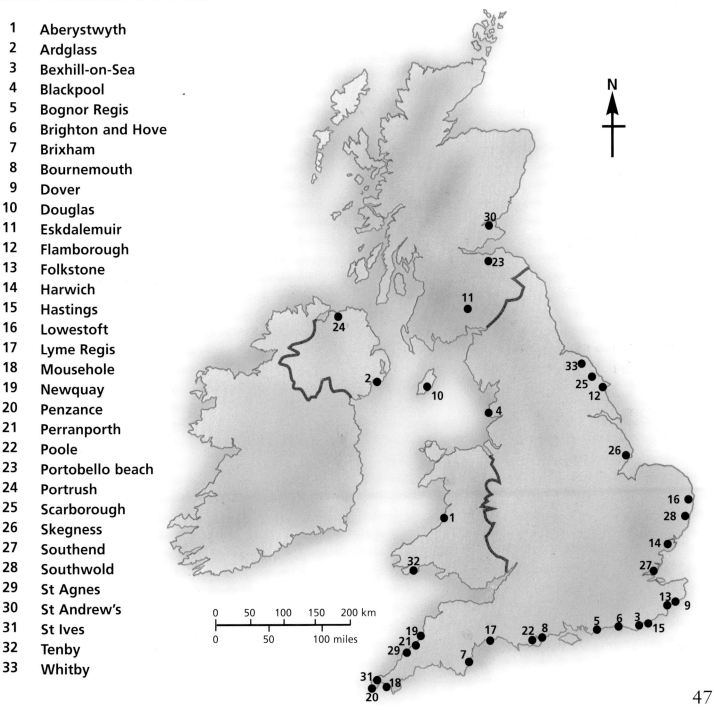

47

Index